IS THAT A FACT?

# Did President Grant Really Get a Ticket for Speeding in a Horse-Drawn Carriage?

## And Other Questions about U.S. Presidents

SANDY DONOVAN

ILLUSTRATIONS BY COLIN W. THOMPSON

LERNER PUBLICATIONS COMPANY

Minneapolis

# Contents

Perhaps you've heard beliefs like these about the U.S. presidents:

George Washington chopped down his father's cherry tree! Millard Fillmore installed the White House's first bathtub!

But are these beliefs true? Is there anything to the stories you've heard? Come along with us as we explore these old beliefs and more. Find out whether the stories and sayings you've heard about U.S. presidents are

**FACT** OR **FICTION!**

# Did Young George Washington Really Chop Down His Father's Cherry Tree?

**PROBABLY NOT. But this might be the most famous myth about a president.**

According to the myth, George got a new hatchet (a small ax) when he was six. He was so excited about his new hatchet that he started chopping. Soon he had chopped down a small cherry tree in his family's yard. When his father asked him if he knew who killed the cherry tree, George admitted that he had done it. George thought he would get in trouble for chopping down the tree. But instead, his father rewarded him for telling the truth.

This story first appeared in 1800, in a book about George Washington's life by Mason Weems. It makes a great point about how important it is to tell the truth. The problem is that there's no evidence it ever really happened.

At the time, George Washington had been dead for only one year. He'd been a beloved president. When he commanded the Continental Army during the Revolutionary War (1775–1783), he showed courage and bravery. In 1789 he became the new nation's first president. Weems must have thought the public would love to read stories about how Washington was honest and brave as a child. And it seems he was right. His story about the cherry tree has been repeated thousands of times.

# Did James Monroe Live Most of His Life with a Bullet in His Shoulder?

**YES.** For fifty-five years, he carried around a bullet in his shoulder from the Revolutionary War. Ouch!

This portrait of President James Monroe was painted in about 1817.

The future president was just seventeen years old when the war broke out. A year later, Monroe joined the Continental Army to fight against the British. Soon after joining, he was wounded at the Battle of Trenton. An enemy bullet grazed the left side of his chest and hit his shoulder.

Monroe's wound was deep, and he bled a lot. In fact, he could have bled to death. Luckily, a doctor on the scene knew how to stop the bleeding. He stuck his index finger into the wound. The pressure of his finger stopped Monroe from losing any more blood.

Later, doctors tried to remove the bullet from Monroe's shoulder. But when they tried to find it, they couldn't. It had lodged too deeply in his shoulder. They had to leave the bullet where it was. You might think that having a bullet lodged in his shoulder would keep Monroe out of battle. But it didn't. In less than three months, he was back in the war.

More than forty years later, in 1817, Monroe became the fifth U.S. president. He is remembered for the Monroe Doctrine. In this statement, Monroe warned foreign nations against establishing new colonies in the Americas or interfering with the nations in that part of the world.

## Did You Know?

_Washington Crossing the Delaware River (above)_ is one of the best-known paintings from the Revolutionary War era. It shows General George Washington leading his troops across the Delaware River. They were sneaking up on the enemy at Trenton, New Jersey. Washington is the main figure in the painting. But just to his right is Lieutenant James Monroe, holding the U.S. flag. Monroe would get shot in the shoulder in the upcoming Battle of Trenton.

# Was Andrew Jackson Really Shot Twice While He Was President?

**NOT EXACTLY.** It's true that someone shot at him two times while he was president. But he was never actually hit by a bullet.

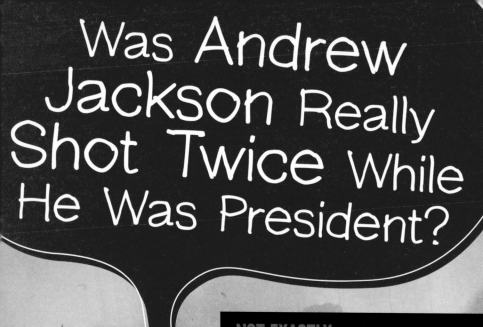

Andrew Jackson leads troops at the Battle of New Orleans in 1815. He became president fourteen years later.

Here's the story. In 1835, President Jackson was walking out of the U.S. Capitol after a funeral. An unemployed housepainter named Richard Lawrence stepped in front of him and fired a pistol. Luckily for Jackson, the pistol misfired. The bullet never left the gun. But then Lawrence pulled out a second pistol. He fired again. But again, the gun misfired! President Jackson escaped a terrible fate twice that day.

Jackson's good fortune was pretty incredible. But what may be even more incredible is that this wasn't the first time that Jackson was almost shot. Jackson was involved in a lot of fights. Indeed, he took part in more than a dozen duels throughout his lifetime. A duel was a fight in which two people agreed beforehand to carry the same type of weapon and follow the same rules. In most duels, the two people fought over a point of honor. In many of Jackson's duels, he fought over his wife, Rachel's, honor. One of those times, in 1806, he actually killed a man who had said something insulting about Rachel. Since it was a duel and duels were considered OK in 1806, Jackson wasn't charged with a crime.

Jackson was born on a settlement in the woods of the Carolinas. During the War of 1812 (1812–1815), he led the U.S. troops in an important battle against the British and became a national hero. During his presidency from 1829 to 1837, Jackson was known for his strong personality. Sometimes he stood up for others. He pushed to give ordinary citizens a greater voice in government. Other times, he bullied people. He helped to remove American Indians from their native homeland.

Rachel Jackson was an honorable woman. She had divorced her first husband, which was unusual at the time. President Jackson often defended her honor because of it.

## How Could That Be?

How did Jackson get so lucky that both of the housepainter's guns misfired? Historians think the hot and humid weather may have been responsible. The moisture in the air may have prevented the gun from firing properly.

# Did Martin Van Buren Invent the Term OK?

**NO.** But most historians agree that the supporters of his 1840 presidential campaign did. In 1840, Martin Van Buren was running for a second term as president. His supporters formed a club called the OK Club. What did OK stand for? The Van Buren supporters didn't tell anyone!

Lots of people had ideas about what the letters meant. Some of Van Buren's opponents joked that OK stood for "Out of Kash," even though they knew that *cash* begins with a C. They wanted to spread the rumor that Van Buren didn't have enough money to run in the election. Other opponents said the initials stood for "oll korrect," because the OK club members weren't smart enough to know how to spell "all correct" correctly. Even though *OK* didn't really stand for "oll correct," the term soon came to mean "all correct," or "everything's all right."

So what did OK *really* stand for? It stood for "Old Kinderhook." That was Van Buren's nickname, because he came from Kinderhook, New York. Did Old Kinderhook do OK in the 1840 election? Nope. He lost his bid for a second term.

This political cartoon from the 1840 presidential election uses the term *OK*.

# Did William Henry Harrison Talk Himself to Death?

**WELL, NO.** But lots of people claim that's what happened.

A large crowd gathers at the U.S. Capitol for William Henry Harrison's inauguration (swearing-in ceremony) in 1841.

Viruses like this one cause the common cold. But people didn't know that in 1841.

Harrison was sworn in as president on March 4, 1841. The day was cold and rainy. And Harrison delivered the longest inauguration speech ever given by a U.S. president. He spoke for two whole hours. He wanted to show everybody how tough he was. So he didn't wear a hat or a coat. After the speech, he rode in a parade through the rainy streets of Washington, D.C.

tried everything they could think of to cure him. They gave him nasty-tasting castor oil. They tried Virginia snakeweed, an ancient cure used by the Seneca people. But nothing helped. Nine days after getting sick, Harrison died at the White House. He had been president for just thirty-one days. This made him the president who talked the longest and served the shortest!

About three weeks later, Harrison came down with a cold. He tried to rest and get better. But he couldn't find any quiet time. As president, he had a busy schedule of events to attend. Soon his cold turned into pneumonia. Doctors

At the time, people believed you could catch a cold from being outside in cold and wet weather. People said that Harrison brought on his own death by talking for two hours in the rain. But these days, doctors know that a cold is caused by a virus, which is a tiny organism. And they know that it rarely takes a person more than a week to get sick from a virus.

## Did You Know?

President Harrison was the first of eight American presidents to die in office. The other seven were Zachary Taylor, Abraham Lincoln, James Garfield, William McKinley, Warren Harding, Franklin D. Roosevelt, and John F. Kennedy.

# Did Millard Fillmore Really Install the White House's First Bathtub?

NO. But this presidential myth has been repeated in dozens of books, magazines, and newspapers.

This illustration shows the White House in the 1850s.

The story was invented by a humor writer named H. L. Mencken. In 1917, Mencken published a story in a New York newspaper about the history of the bathtub. The story was only a joke. But lots of people took it seriously.

Mencken's story claimed that the first bathtub in the United States was built in Cincinnati in 1842. The story also claimed that many Americans were afraid to try out a bathtub. The story said that doctors of the time had warned that taking a bath was unhealthful. They said that it could spread diseases.

But then, Mencken wrote, President Millard Fillmore came to the bathtub's rescue. Fillmore was president from 1850 to 1853. One day, Fillmore was visiting Cincinnati and took a bath in the original Cincinnati tub. He loved the experience, and he became a big fan of the bathtub. Soon he ordered a tub for the White House. And Americans began using bathtubs. If it was all right for the president, it must be all right for other people.

Every part of this story came from Mencken's imagination. But it's been retold as truth hundreds of times. It's been printed in the *Washington Post*. Cable TV's DIY Network featured it. And the Presidential Pet Museum, in Williamsburg, Virginia, repeated it as fact.

H. L. Mencken

Millard Fillmore

## What's the Real Story?

Records show that President James Monroe bought a tin bathtub for the White House in 1825. It cost about twenty-five dollars. But at the time, there was no running water in the White House bathrooms. Monroe's bathwater had to be heated and poured into the tub. In 1834, President Andrew Jackson introduced running water to White House bathrooms.

# Did Abraham Lincoln Really Walk Twenty Miles to School Each Day Barefoot?

**PROBABLY NOT.** But boy, do people like to tell this story. The idea behind it is that the young Abe Lincoln faced great hardships. And that was certainly true. Abe probably would have walked 20 miles (32 kilometers) to school if he'd had the chance. But he spent most of his days working on his father's farm or clearing the surrounding forest.

Abraham Lincoln was born on this land in Kentucky. He faced many hardships throughout his childhood—but he probably never walked to school barefoot!

Abe Lincoln was born on a farm in Kentucky in 1809. He and his sister, Sarah, enjoyed themselves on the farm. But when Abe was seven, his father moved the family to Indiana. At the time, the area was wilderness. For the first winter, Abe and his family lived in a shack with only three walls. Soon Abe's father built a log cabin. Abe helped his father chop down trees for the cabin.

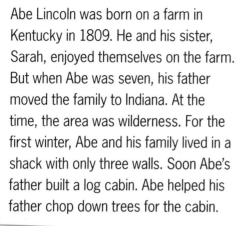

This painting from the early 1800s shows Abraham Lincoln as a boy.

Less than two years after the Lincolns moved to Indiana, Abe's mother died. A year later, Abe's father married again. Abe grew close to his stepmother. She encouraged him to learn to read and write. Abe loved to learn. He did go to school sometimes. In fact, by the time he was seventeen, he had attended five schools. A couple of those were about 5 miles (8 km) from his home. But Lincoln didn't have much formal schooling. All together, he spent less than eighteen months attending school.

Lincoln made the most of the schools he did attend. He spent whatever free time he had practicing his reading, writing, and math. Unfortunately, his family didn't own books, pencils, or even candles to provide light for reading. So Abe practiced writing with pieces of charcoal on slats of wood. He used the light from the family's cooking fire to see. And he borrowed books whenever he could. His hard work paid off. Lincoln became a lawyer in his twenties. He served as the sixteenth president of the United States from 1861 to 1865.

Abraham Lincoln posed for this photograph in 1864 during his presidency.

# Is It True That Andrew Johnson Never Attended School?

**YES!** Andrew Johnson was born in 1808 in Raleigh, North Carolina. His father died before Andrew was four years old. His mother had to take care of Andrew and his brother by herself. She had no money to send them to school. Instead, she sent Andrew to live and work with a tailor (somebody who makes or repairs clothes). This was called an apprenticeship. It was a common arrangement for young people to learn skills without going to school. As a tailor, Johnson would be able to support himself.

Although Johnson didn't go to school, he did learn to read and write. He learned first from the customers in the tailor's shop. They would read to him while he worked on their clothes. Some of them gave him books. He taught himself how to read.

**Andrew Johnson**

**Eliza McCardle Johnson**

When Johnson was eighteen, he married Eliza McCardle. She had been to school, and she helped her husband with his writing and reading. She also taught him math. After that, Johnson's lack of schooling never slowed him down.

When he was in his twenties, he was elected mayor of Greeneville, Tennessee. Before long, he was elected to the Tennessee House of Representatives. He later served as a congressman and then a senator in the U.S. Congress. In 1861, while Johnson was a senator, eleven southern states left the Union. The southern states were afraid that President Abraham Lincoln's administration would become too powerful. They thought he would force them to give up the practice of slavery. Johnson was the only senator from the South who did not quit the Senate. The Civil War (1861–1865) began that summer.

In 1864 Johnson was elected as President Abraham Lincoln's vice president. When Lincoln was killed in April 1865, Johnson became president. During his presidency, the southern states rejoined the Union. Johnson was nearly removed from office because many thought he was too easy on the defeated southern states.

This is the tailor shop in Greeneville, Tennessee, where Andrew Johnson worked and began a career in politics instead of attending school. This photograph was taken in the early 1900s.

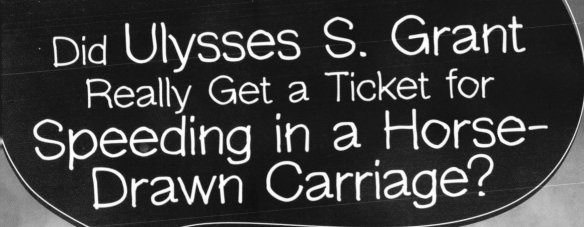

# Did Ulysses S. Grant Really Get a Ticket for Speeding in a Horse-Drawn Carriage?

This engraving of Ulysses S. Grant was created in the 1860s.

**HE DID.** He was speeding through the streets of Washington in his one-horse carriage one day. A police officer pulled him over. Once the officer realized it was the president, he didn't want to give him a ticket. But President Grant insisted that he shouldn't get special treatment. He paid the fine on the spot. Later, he sent the police officer a letter telling him what a good job he did.

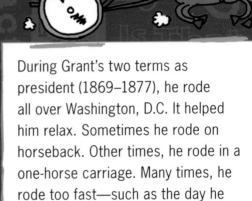

Grant loved riding horses his entire life. When he was a child, he rode and trained horses with more skill than most adults. When Grant went to college at the U.S. Military Academy at West Point, he won awards for his horseback riding.

He became a military commander during the Civil War. Grant's riding skills probably helped him win many victories for the Union. In 1864, President Lincoln made Grant the general in chief of the Union armies.

During Grant's two terms as president (1869–1877), he rode all over Washington, D.C. It helped him relax. Sometimes he rode on horseback. Other times, he rode in a one-horse carriage. Many times, he rode too fast—such as the day he got that ticket!

This photograph shows a man driving a horse-drawn carriage in the late 1800s.

# Did Grover Cleveland Have Secret Surgery on a Private Yacht?

**YES!** Long before the days of the Internet and television, presidents knew how to keep away from the prying eyes of the press.

Grover Cleveland had his surgery on board the *Oneida* in 1893. In the early 1900s, the U.S. Navy made it into a tugboat.

Grover Cleveland began his second term as president in March 1893. About three months later, doctors found a tumor in his mouth. This lump was the size of a silver dollar. The doctors were sure it was cancer. They told the president he needed an operation to remove it. President Cleveland wanted to have the operation. But he was worried about what the American people would think. If they knew he had cancer, would they think he was too sick to be president? He decided to keep quiet about the cancer. And he arranged for a secret surgery.

Grover Cleveland posed for this picture in the 1890s.

The president announced that he would take a short vacation in early July. He would sail to his summer home in Massachusetts on his friend's yacht. On June 30, he boarded the yacht in New York City. Four doctors and a dentist boarded when no one would see them. The next morning, as the yacht sailed up the East River, the doctors operated on the president.

Everybody was nervous about keeping the operation secret. When the yacht sailed past New York City's Bellevue Hospital, all the doctors hid in the boat's cabin. They didn't want to be seen by any doctors who might happen to be looking out a window of the hospital.

And the operation? It was a success. President Cleveland lived for another fifteen years. He died in 1908 at the age of seventy-one.

## Was Benjamin Harrison's Nickname Really the Human Iceberg?

**YES, IT WAS.** From a distance, people admired Harrison's personality. But up close, he could be stiff. He was described as cold because he didn't like to make small talk with people. Even when he was introduced to someone, often he would barely utter a word as he shook the person's hand. This kind of behavior didn't help his reputation as a cold person. People began saying he was so cold that he was like an iceberg. Soon the name stuck, and Harrison's official nickname became the Human Iceberg.

There was another reason people thought Harrison was unfriendly. Sometimes he refused to shake hands with people if he wasn't wearing gloves. Harrison had a great fear of germs. He didn't want to touch other people's hands and get their germs.

This photo of Benjamin Harrison was taken in the late 1800s. Benjamin Harrison, our twenty-third president, was the grandson of William Henry Harrison, our ninth president.

Harrison was president from 1889 to 1893. He is best remembered for signing the Sherman Antitrust Act into law. This law made it illegal for large companies to form partnerships that would be unfair to their competitors. By preventing groups of companies from becoming too powerful, the Sherman Antitrust Act protected American consumers.

## Did You Know?

Harrison's fear of germs may have been well founded. Eight years after he left the presidency, he caught a cold. That was in February 1901. One month later, he died of complications from the illness.

# Is It True That William Howard Taft Weighed More Than an Elephant?

**HE DIDN'T WEIGH MORE THAN A FULL-GROWN ELEPHANT.** But he definitely weighed more than a baby elephant. When Taft was elected president in 1909, he weighed 332 pounds (151 kilograms).

At the time, being very overweight was sometimes considered a status symbol. If you weighed a lot, you might have a desk job. You probably weren't doing hard physical work, such as farming or building houses. And you obviously had plenty to eat. Nevertheless, the press and other Americans made fun of Taft's extra pounds.

As you can imagine, Taft had a few health problems from being so overweight. He found it hard to get around. He also had trouble sleeping. Doctors thought that his extra weight made it hard for him to breathe. He woke up constantly all night long. Of course, this meant he was very tired most days. Taft was famous for falling asleep during the day. He fell asleep during important meetings, during dinner, while playing cards, and even while being driven in an open car during a presidential parade.

According to one story, Taft's extra weight got him stuck in the White House bathtub once. He had to be pulled out, and he later ordered an extra-large bathtub for the White House. It was big enough for four regular-size men to take a bath at the same time.

Throughout Taft's time as president, his wife, Helen, and doctors warned him that he needed to lose weight. But he found it difficult. Finally, after leaving the White House in 1913, he lost almost 80 pounds (36 kg) in less than two years. His health improved, and he lived for another seventeen years. He died at the age of seventy-two.

## Did You Know?

Taft had other claims to fame in addition to being the heaviest president. He was also the first president to own a car at the White House. And he was the last president to have a mustache.

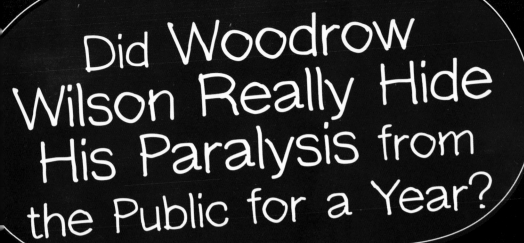

# Did Woodrow Wilson Really Hide His Paralysis from the Public for a Year?

**YES!** Hard as it may be to believe, Wilson spent part of his presidency in a wheelchair—and the public never knew it.

President Wilson and his wife, Edith, pose for a picture at his desk after his recovery in 1920.

Wilson's presidency began in 1913. He was already in poor health when he took office. He had probably suffered several strokes. A stroke causes blood to temporarily stop flowing to a person's brain. As a result of these strokes, Wilson lost his sense of touch in his right hand. In 1919, during his second term as president, Wilson suffered another stroke. This one paralyzed him on his left side. He couldn't move his left arm or leg. He also couldn't see out of his left eye.

After his stroke, the president had to use a wheelchair for a while. After several months, he could walk with a cane. But he didn't want the American people to know he was partly paralyzed. He kept his illness a secret from almost everyone. Only his wife and a few other members of the government knew. Even the vice president didn't know that the president had suffered a paralyzing stroke!

Stress may have contributed to Wilson's stroke. Wilson was president during a challenging time. The year after he became president, World War I (1914–1918) began. In 1917, Wilson led the United States into that war, even though many Americans objected. After the war, Wilson came up with the idea for a League of Nations. This group made up of different countries would work to settle arguments between countries. Wilson hoped it would prevent another world war. But a lot of Americans didn't want their country to join the league. They wanted the U.S. government to focus on its own country.

President Wilson felt strongly that the world needed a League of Nations. He collapsed while he was traveling around the country making speeches about his idea. The League of Nations did become a reality, but the United States never joined.

The leaders of the winning countries of World War I meet in France in 1919. Wilson is on the far right.

# Did Calvin Coolidge Really Have a Pet Raccoon in the White House?

**HE DID!** President Coolidge and his wife, Grace, had dozens of pets. These included cats, dogs, birds, a donkey, and, yes, even a raccoon.

Grace Coolidge shows her family's pet raccoon to a group of children at the White House in 1927.

The raccoon was actually a present to the Coolidges. But it wasn't supposed to be a pet. Instead, a voter in Mississippi had sent it for the Coolidges to eat on Thanksgiving Day! But the Coolidges were big animal lovers. Instead of eating the raccoon, they adopted her. They named her Rebecca.

The Coolidges had a house built for Rebecca on the White House lawn. When Rebecca was outside, she was tied to a chain. But inside the White House, she could roam wherever she wanted. One of her favorite activities was using the bathtub as a swimming pool. Mrs. Coolidge would fill the tub with a few inches of water and give Rebecca a bar of soap to play with. President Coolidge liked to play with Rebecca too. He sometimes wrapped her around his shoulders while he was working.

Rebecca escaped from the White House grounds a few times. But someone always found her and brought her home. Still, the Coolidges were afraid a car would hit her. They decided the White House wasn't safe enough for her. They donated her to the National Zoo, in Washington, D.C. Rebecca adjusted well and seemed happy living there for the rest of her life.

## Did You Know?

President Coolidge didn't just love real animals. He loved fake ones too. He had an electric horse installed in the White House. He rode the horse every day!

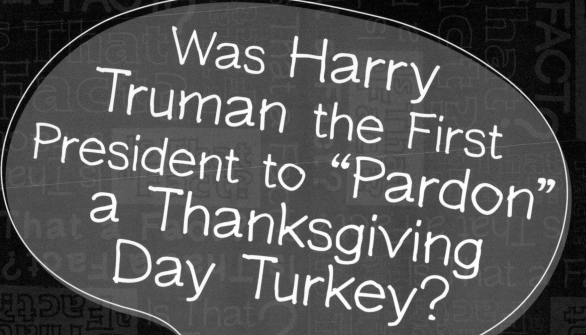

Was Harry Truman the First President to "Pardon" a Thanksgiving Day Turkey?

**NOPE.** Presidents do have a formal ceremony every year in which they pardon a turkey. The president announces that the turkey will get to live in a petting zoo instead of ending up as Thanksgiving dinner. But Harry Truman didn't start this tradition.

President Truman receives a turkey for Thanksgiving in 1949.

Still, there is a turkey connection to Truman's presidency. And it may explain how this myth got started. Here are the facts.

In December 1947, the National Turkey Federation (yes, there is such a group!) sent a live turkey to the White House. It was a gift for President Truman and his family to eat on Christmas Day. The Trumans ate the turkey. Sometime over the next thirty years, the turkey group began sending a live turkey to the White House every November. It became the official White House Thanksgiving turkey.

OFFICIAL WHITE HOUSE TURKEY

Somewhere along the way, White House workers began sending the bird to a farm or a zoo each year instead of cooking it for dinner. And in 1989, President George H. W. Bush decided to hold a formal ceremony to pardon the White House bird. So he—not Truman—was the first president to ceremonially pardon a turkey.

Every year since then, the president of the United States has held a ceremony on the White House lawn to pardon the turkey. Then the bird is sent to live out the rest of its life at a nearby petting zoo or farm. But it's usually a pretty short life. Turkeys that are raised for food get so fat that they live for only a few years.

President George H. W. Bush pardons a turkey in 1990.

33

# Was Dwight D. Eisenhower's Dog Kicked Out of the White House?

**YES.** The reason? It was a classic dog mistake. The dog peed on the rug.

First Lady Mamie Eisenhower and her granddaughter Barbara Anne play with the Eisenhowers' dog, Heidi, outside of the White House in 1958.

Unfortunately for the dog, this wasn't just any rug. The rug was in a part of the White House where the president greeted foreign leaders. And it was valued at about $20,000. The White House cleaning staff tried to remove the stain. But they couldn't. They had to remove the rug instead.

Eisenhower had always been a dog lover. When he became president in 1953, he and his wife, Mamie, got a dog to live at the White House with them. The dog was a Weimaraner named Heidi. Weimaraners are German hunting dogs. They were popular family dogs in the 1950s because they were known for being well behaved. The Eisenhowers adored Heidi. But when Heidi made her big mistake, Eisenhower decided that maybe the White House wasn't the best home for her. So Heidi was booted. She went to live at the Eisenhowers' farm near Gettysburg, Pennsylvania.

President Eisenhower plays golf on the White House lawn in 1953.

## Did You Know?

Eisenhower enjoyed sharing his home with his dog, Heidi. But he didn't feel the same way about the squirrels on the White House lawn. These critters interfered with his golf practice, and the president loved to play golf. So he asked White House workers to trap the squirrels and remove them from the White House grounds.

## Did George H. W. Bush Really Go on a Bombing Mission While His Plane Was on Fire?

George H. W. Bush sits in the VT-51 Avenger that he used for missions during World War II (1939–1945).

**NOT EXACTLY.** During World War II, Bush flew fifty-eight combat missions. He flew planes that dropped torpedoes over the Japanese forces. One day while attacking an enemy base on an island in the Pacific Ocean, Bush's plane was hit. His engine caught on fire. Bush and the two other crew members kept flying. And they did release some bombs before heading back toward their aircraft carrier. But they didn't begin a new bombing mission.

President George H. W. Bush showed bravery during World War II, but there was one enemy he couldn't face: broccoli! He was famous for refusing to eat this healthful vegetable.

George H. W. Bush poses for his official presidential portrait in the early 1990s.

Before the men could reach the aircraft carrier, they had to bail out of their burning plane. The other two crew members died, but Bush survived. He floated for hours in the ocean. Then a U. S. submarine rescued him. Bush was awarded the Distinguished Flying Cross for bravery during war.

Bush had enlisted in the navy on his eighteenth birthday. The United States had just entered World War II, and Bush wanted to serve his country instead of going to college. Days before he turned nineteen, he became the youngest U.S. Navy pilot, up to that time.

After World War II ended, Bush went to college. He moved to Texas and became successful in the oil business. In 1980, he was elected vice president of the United States and served alongside President Ronald Reagan. Eight years later, Bush became the forty-first U.S. president. He served from 1989 to 1993. When Iraq invaded the nation of Kuwait in 1990, Bush sent U.S. troops into the region. With the help of troops from other nations, the United States forced Iraq to withdraw.

# GLOSSARY

**apprenticeship:** an arrangement for learning a trade or craft by working with a skilled person

**Civil War:** the war fought in the United States from 1861 to 1865 between the Northern states and the Southern states

**duel:** a fight where two people agreed beforehand to carry the same weapons and follow the same rules

**graze:** to scrape the surface off skin

**hatchet:** an ax with a short handle

**inauguration:** the ceremony of swearing in a public official

**misfire:** when a gun fails to shoot a bullet or a shell

**mission:** a special job or task. In the armed forces, troops or crews complete missions.

**opponent:** someone who is against another person in a fight, a contest, or an election

**pardon:** to forgive or to spare from punishment

**pneumonia:** a serious disease that fills the lungs with fluid and makes breathing difficult

**reputation:** a person's worth or character, as judged by others

**Revolutionary War:** the war fought from 1775 to 1783, in which the thirteen colonies won their independence from Great Britain

**status symbol:** a possession or a quality that symbolizes a person's rank or position in society

**torpedo:** an underwater missile that explodes when it hits a target

**tumor:** an abnormal lump or mass of tissue in the body

**virus:** a tiny organism that invades the cells of living things and forces them to produce new viruses

**yacht:** a large, often fancy boat used for pleasure or racing

## SELECTED BIBLIOGRAPHY

C-SPAN. *"Welcome to American Presidents: Life Portraits."* American Presidents. 2009. http://www. americanpresidents.org/ (December 23, 2009).

DeGregorio, William A. *The Complete Book of the U.S. Presidents*, 6th ed. Fort Lee, NJ: Barricade Books, 2005.

Van Tassel, David D. *"The Legend Maker."* American Heritage 13, no. 2 (February 1962): 58–59, 89–94.

The White House. *"The Presidents."* Whitehouse.gov. N.d. http://www .whitehouse.gov/about/presidents/ (December 23, 2009).

Whitney, David C. *The American Presidents*. Garden City, NY: Doubleday, 1975.

## FURTHER READING

Barber, James, and Amy Pastan. *Smithsonian Presidents and First Ladies*. New York: DK Publishing, 2002. This illustrated book provides quick facts and interesting trivia about the U.S. presidents and their wives.

Bausum, Ann. *Our Country's Presidents: All You Need to Know about the Presidents, from George Washington to Barack Obama*. Washington, D.C.: National Geographic, 2009. This fun book gives great information on all our nation's leaders.

Davis, Kathryn Gibbs. *Wackiest White House Pets*. New York: Scholastic Press, 2004. Check out this book to get the scoop on more than two hundred years of presidential pets.

Presidents: CyberSleuth Kids http://cybersleuth-kids.com/sleuth/ History/US_History/Presidents/index .htm CyberSleuth Kids helps you find websites with plenty of presidential facts.

Presidents: The Secret History http://pbskids.org/wayback/prez/ secrets/index.html This website, sponsored by PBS, reveals many fascinating secrets of U.S. presidents. You'll recognize a few from this book. But there are many more.

Waxman, Laura Hamilton. *Woodrow Wilson*. Minneapolis: Lerner Publications Company, 2006. Learn more about Woodrow Wilson's presidency. Find out how he persuaded other nations to establish a League of Nations but failed to convince his fellow Americans to join.

# INDEX

ACKNOWLEDGMENTS
The images in this book are used with the permission of:
© Hulton Collection/Hulton Archive/Getty Images, p. 1;
© National Maritime Museum, London/The Image Works, pp. 2 (both), 6; © Duncan Noakes/Dreamstime.com, pp. 3 (top), 26; AP Photo/James A. Finley, pp. 3 (bottom), 32; © Baloncici/Dreamstime.com, p. 4; © Cepixx/Dreamstime.com, p. 5; © SuperStock/SuperStock, p. 6 (inset); © Time & Life Pictures/Getty Images, p. 7; Library of Congress, pp. 8 (LC-USZC4-6221), 9 (LC-USZ62-100102), 10 (LC-DIG-pga-02634), 11 (LC-USZ62-10497), 12 (LC-USZ62-58550), 13 (LC-USZ62-13009), 15 (bottom, LC-USZ62-13013), 17 (right, LC-DIG-ppmsca-19211), 19 (top, LC-USZ62-13017), 19 (bottom, LC-USZ62-25821), 20 (LC-DIG-pga-02645), 26 (inset, LC-DIG-hec-15145), 28 (LC-DIG-ppmsca-13425), 30–31 (LC-DIG-npcc-16726); © Biophoto Associates/Photo Researchers, Inc., pp. 12–13; © Stock Montage/SuperStock, pp. 14–15; © MPI/Archive Photos/Getty Images, pp. 15 (top), 36–37, 37 (bottom); © Willis D. Vaughn/National Geographic/Getty Images, pp. 16–17; © William Vander Weyde/George Eastman House/Archive Photos/Getty Images, p. 17 (left); The Art Archive, pp. 18–19; © Otto Herschan/Hulton Archive/Getty Images, p. 21; From the www.jsjohnston.org collection, pp. 22–23; © Stock Montage/Archive Photos/Getty Images, p. 23; © Melissa King/Dreamstime.com, pp. 24–25; The Art Archive/Culver Pictures, p. 25; AP Photo, pp. 29, 33 (top); AP Photo/Marcy Nighswander, p. 33 (bottom); © Ed Clark/Time & Life Pictures/Getty Images, p. 34; © Hank Walker/Time & Life Pictures/Getty Images, p. 35 (left); © Sireagle/Dreamstime.com, p. 35 (right); © Openko Dmytro/Dreamstime.com, p. 37 (top).

Front cover: © iStockphoto.com/Terraxplorer (left); © Hulton Collection/Hulton Archive/Getty Images (right); Library of Congress (LC-DIG-cwpbh-03295) (background).

Lerner Publications Company
A division of Lerner Publishing Group, Inc.
241 First Avenue North
Minneapolis, MN 55401 U.S.A.

Website address: www.lernerbooks.com

Library of Congress Cataloging-in-Publication Data

Donovan, Sandra, 1967–
    Did President Grant really get a ticket for speeding in a horse-drawn carriage? : and other questions about U.S. presidents / by Sandy Donovan.
        p.   cm. — (Is that a fact?)
    Includes bibliographical references and index.
    ISBN 978–0–7613–6101–5 (lib. bdg. : alk. paper)
    1. Presidents—United States—Miscellanea—Juvenile literature. 2. Presidents—United States—Biography—Juvenile literature.  I. Title.
E176.1.D694 2011
973.09'9—dc22                                    2010028897

Manufactured in the United States of America
1 – CG – 12/31/10